STIRLING · ALLOA

BRIDGE OF ALLAN · DUNBLANE

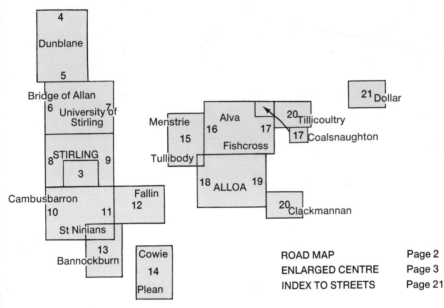

ROAD MAP	Page 2
ENLARGED CENTRE	Page 3
INDEX TO STREETS	Page 21

Every effort has been made to verify the accuracy of information in this book but the publishers cannot accept responsibility for expense or loss caused by any error or omission. Information that will be of assistance to the user of the maps will be welcomed.

The representation of a road, track or footpath on the maps in this atlas is no evidence of the existence of a right of way.

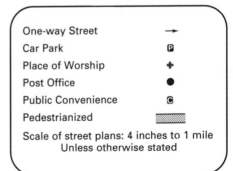

One-way Street	→
Car Park	🅿
Place of Worship	✚
Post Office	●
Public Convenience	🅲
Pedestrianized	▨

Scale of street plans: 4 inches to 1 mile
Unless otherwise stated

Street plans prepared and published by ESTATE PUBLICATIONS, Bridewell House, TENTERDEN, KENT, and based upon the ORDNANCE SURVEY mapping with the permission of The Controller of H. M. Stationery Office.

The publishers acknowledge the co-operation of the local authorities of towns represented in this atlas.

Estate Publications 476 B   ISBN 0 86084 879 5   © Crown Copyright 398713

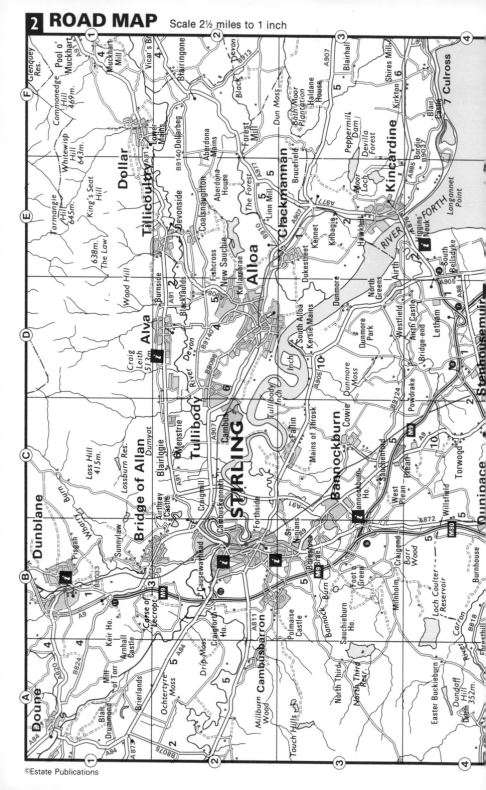

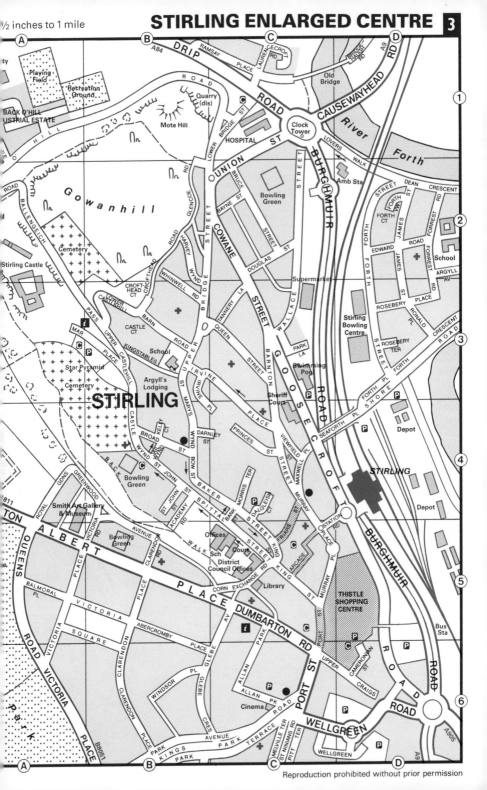

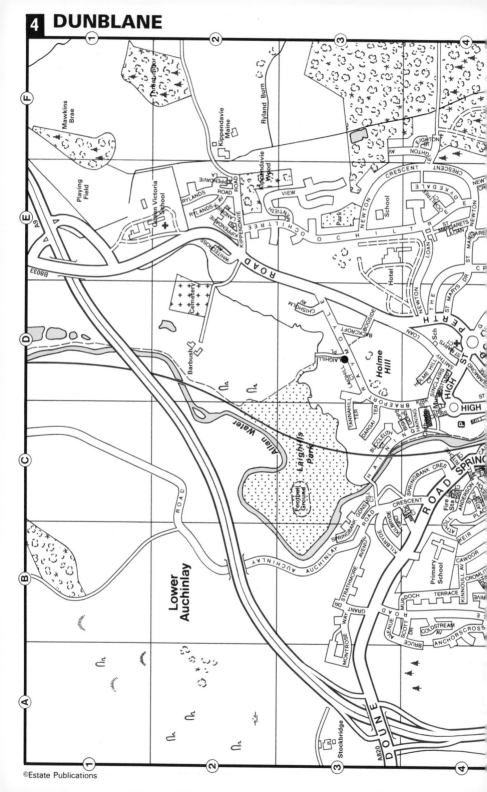

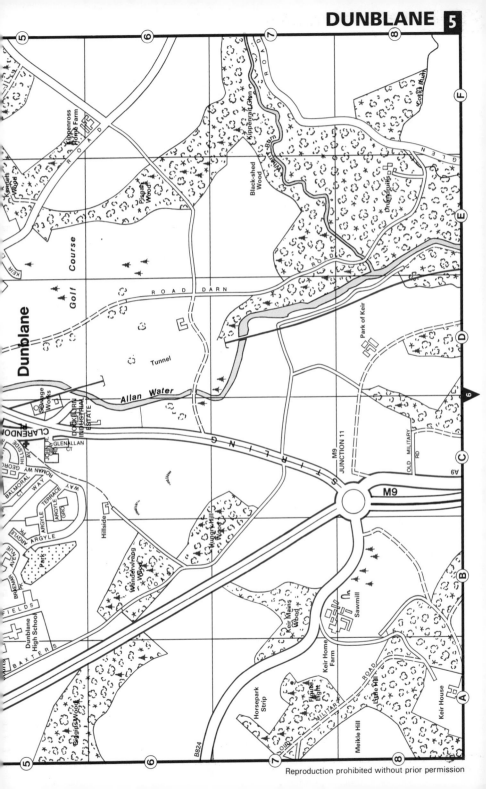

Dunblane

Kippenross Home Farm

Mentirs Wood

Pisgah Wood

Black-shed Wood

Kippenrait Glen

Craighgulls

Golf Course

ROAD DARN

Park of Keir

Tunnel

Allan Water

Sewage Works

DOGHILLH INDUSTRIAL ESTATE

GLENALLAN CT

CLARENDON

GEORGE ROMAN WY

HILLSIDE

BALMORAL CT

ARGYLE TERRACE GRO

ARGYLE WAY

ARGYLE PK

ARGYLE AVE

Park

BREMAR AVE

FIELDS

Dunblane High School

Muirs

BAXTERS

Biggins Wood

Hillside

Wanderknowg Wood

Hungry Hill Wood

M9 JUNCTION 11

OLD MILITARY RD

A9

M9

Keir Mauns Wood

Sawmill

Keir Home Farm

Horsepark Strip

Found Eight

MILITAR

Lime Kiln

ROAD

Keir House

Meikle Hill

B824

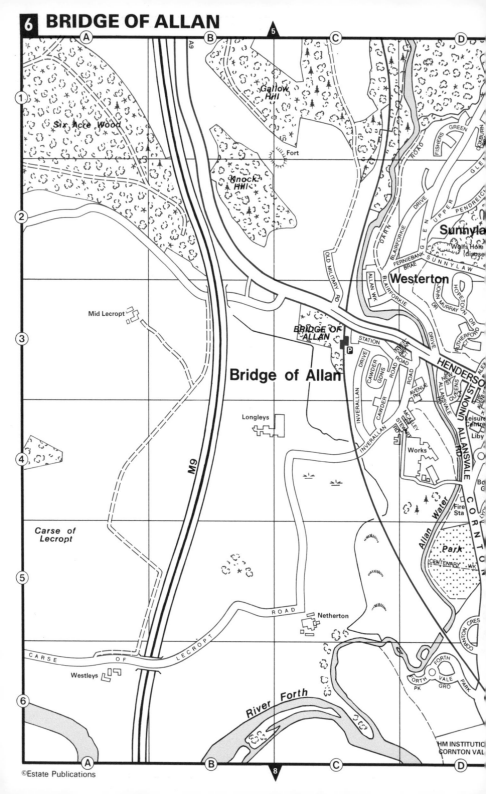

6 BRIDGE OF ALLAN

©Estate Publications

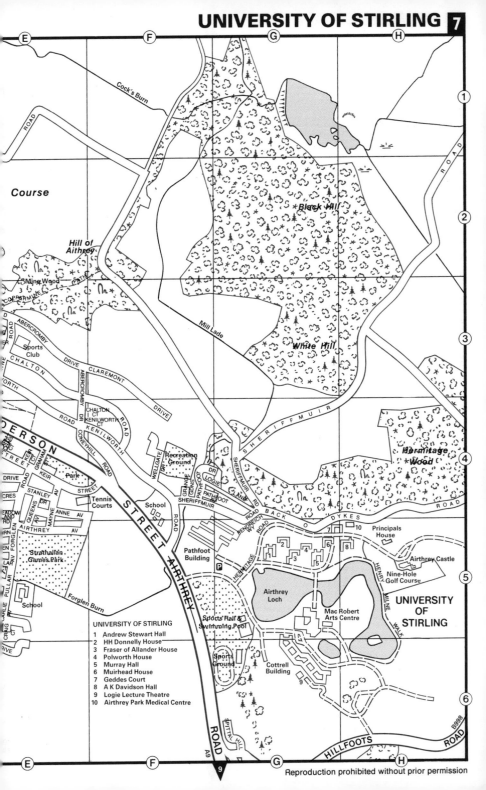

E F G H

1
2
3
4
5
6

Cock's Burn

ROAD

Course

Black Hill

Hill of Aithrey

Ming Wood

COPPERMINE

Mill Lade

White Hill

Sports Club

ABERCROMBY

DRIVE

CHALTON

CLAREMONT DRIVE

ABERCROMBY DR

CHALTON CT
KENILWORTH CT

ROAD

KENILWORTH

CONEYHILL ROAD

WELLGATE

SHERIFFMUIR

Hermitage Wood

ROAD

DERSON

STREET

GRAHAM

KEIR

PARK

Park

STANLEY

MAYNE

STREET

QUEENS DR

AIRTHREY AV

ANNE AV

Tennis Courts

School

Recreation Ground

DR
LOGIE

GRANGE GDNS

PATHFOOT

SHERIFFMUIR

PATHFOOT

CLANE

SHERIFFMUIR RD

BENREOCH ROAD

BACK O DYKES

Principals House

7 10

Airthrey Castle

Nine-Hole Golf Course

ROAD

Strathallan Games Park

MEADOW AND RD

FORGLEN

AV

CRAIG CARLILE PULLAR

DRIVE

School

Forglen Burn

STREET

AIRTHREY

ROAD

Pathfoot Building

P

HERMITAGE ROAD

2

3

4

6

5

8

HENRY MILNE WALK

UNIVERSITY OF STIRLING

Airthrey Loch

Mac Robert Arts Centre

Sports Hall & Swimming Pool

Sports Ground

Cottrell Building

Logie Lecture Theatre

9

SPITTAL HILL

UNIVERSITY OF STIRLING
1 Andrew Stewart Hall
2 HH Donnelly House
3 Fraser of Allander House
4 Polworth House
5 Murray Hall
6 Muirhead House
7 Geddes Court
8 A K Davidson Hall
9 Logie Lecture Theatre
10 Airthrey Park Medical Centre

ROAD

A9

HILLFOOTS ROAD

B998

E F G H

9

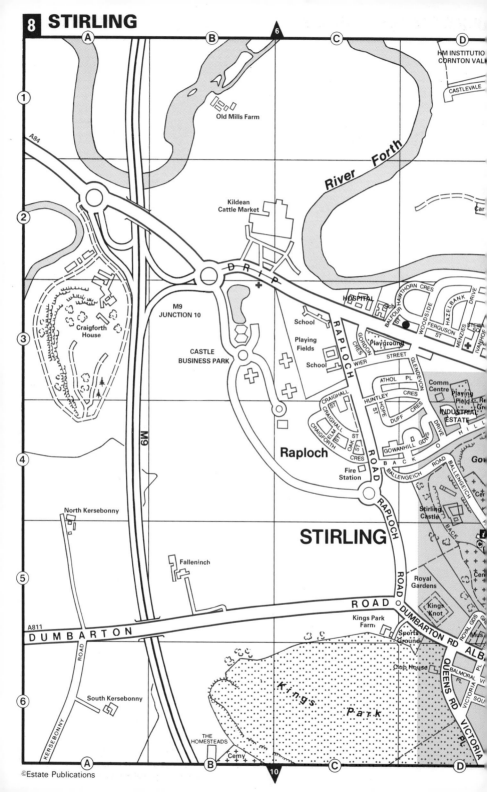

A   B   6   C   D

1

Old Mills Farm

HM INSTITUTIO
CORNTON VAL
CASTLEVALE

A84

River Forth

Car

2

Kildean
Cattle Market

DRIP

M9
JUNCTION 10

HOSPITAL

Sch
HAWTHORN CRES
BALFOUR
WOODSIDE
HAZELBANK
DRIVE
MENZIES
STEW
SQU
IVANHOE

Craigforth
House

School

Playing
Fields

School

R A P L O C H

FERGUSON
ST

Playground
STREET

GORDON
CRES
WIER
GLENDEVON

3

CASTLE
BUSINESS
PARK

ATHOL PL
CRES
HUNTLEY
ST
HOPE
DUFF CRES

Comm
Centre

Playing
Field Re
Gr

INDUSTRIAL
ESTATE

CRAIGHALL
ST
CRAIGHALL
CRAIGFORTH

GOWANHILL GDNS

ROAD
O

HILL

Gow

4

Raploch

CRES

BACK
BALLENGEICH

ROAD

BALLENGEICH

Ce

Fire
Station

DRIVE

Stirling
Castle

BACK

C

North Kersebonny

RAPLOCH

STIRLING

Cer

5

Falleninch

ROAD

Royal
Gardens

Kings
Knot

Cer
Vi

DUMBARTON RD

ROAD

A811

DUMBARTON

ROAD

KERSEBONNY

Kings Park
Farm

Sports
Ground

ROYAL GDS GR

Mus

ALB

BALMORAL
PL

QUEENS RD

VICTORIA
PL

6

South Kersebonny

Club House

King's   Park

VICTORIA
PL

THE
HOMESTEADS
Cemy

A   B   10   C   D

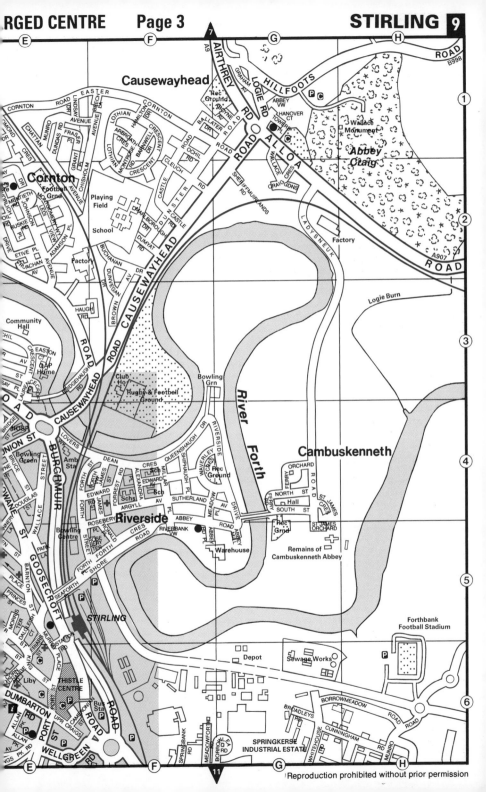

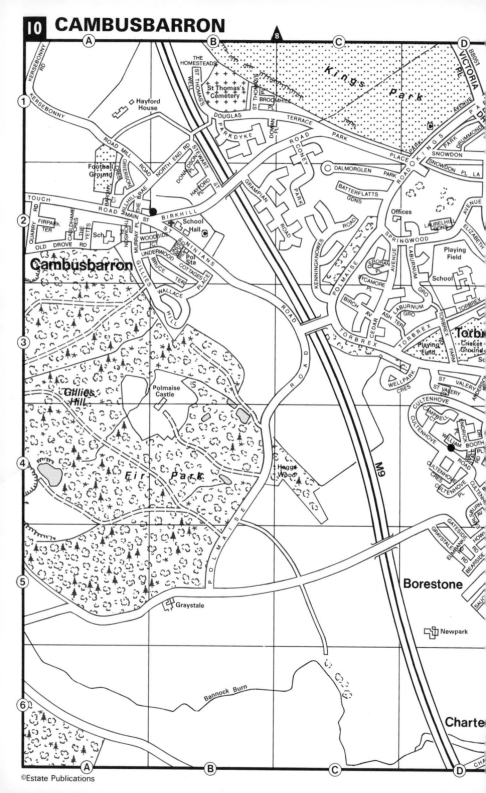

10 CAMBUSBARRON

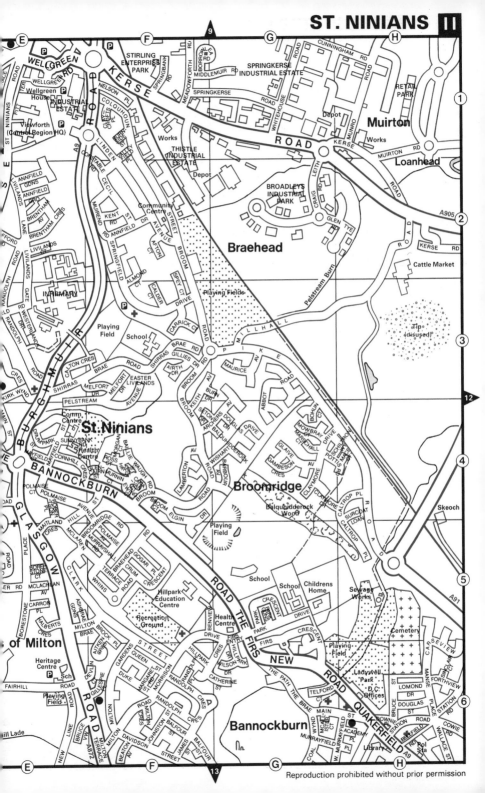

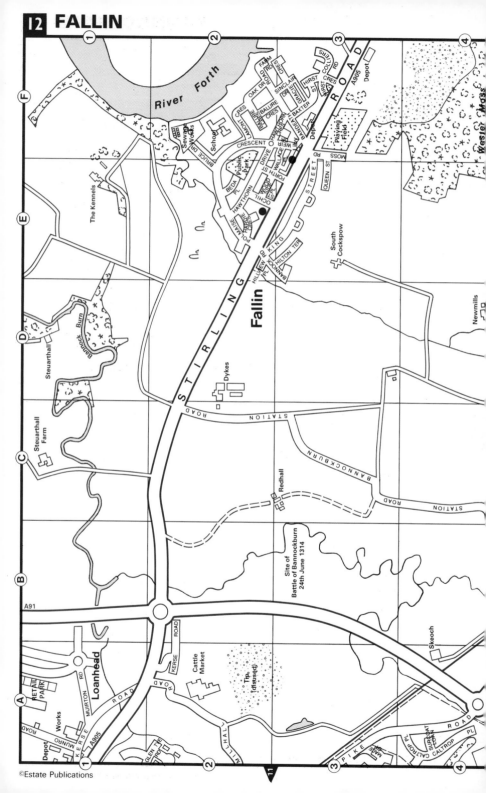

12 FALLIN

River Forth

Wester Moss

The Kennels

Steuarthall

Bannock Burn

Steuarthall Farm

STIRLING ROAD

Fallin

Sewage Works

School

Public Park

CRESCENT

BRUCE DRIVE

FARM DR
OAK DR
CROFTS
SINCLAIR
HIRST ST
GRACIE
BANNOCK
BAXTER
WALLACE ST
FORTH
WEIR
BALLVRE CRES
LABURNUM CRES
HAWTHORN CRES
BEDA PL
POLMAISE CRES
HAWTHORN TERRACE
OCHIL
WOOD

COLLINS CRES
CRES
A905
Depot

Depot

ROAD
A905

QUEEN ST
MOSS RD
HILTON TER

Playing Field

South Cockspow

Newmills

HILLVIEW RD
KING
BANNOCK ST
STREET

Dykes

STATION ROAD
ROAD

BANNOCKBURN

Redhall

STATION ROAD

Site of
Battle of Bannockburn
24th June 1314

Skeoch

A91

Loanhead

RETAIL PARK

Works

Depot

MUNRO ROAD
KERSE ROAD
KERSE ROAD
MUIRTON RD
A905

GLEN TER

Cattle Market

Tp.
(disused)

MILLHALL

PIKE ROAD

MADE
SURGOAT CALTROP PL
SURGEON CALTROP PL

©Estate Publications

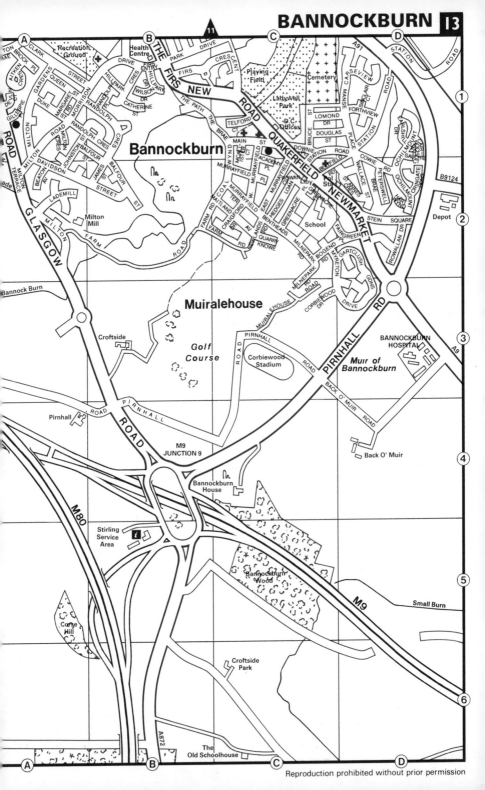

BANNOCKBURN 13

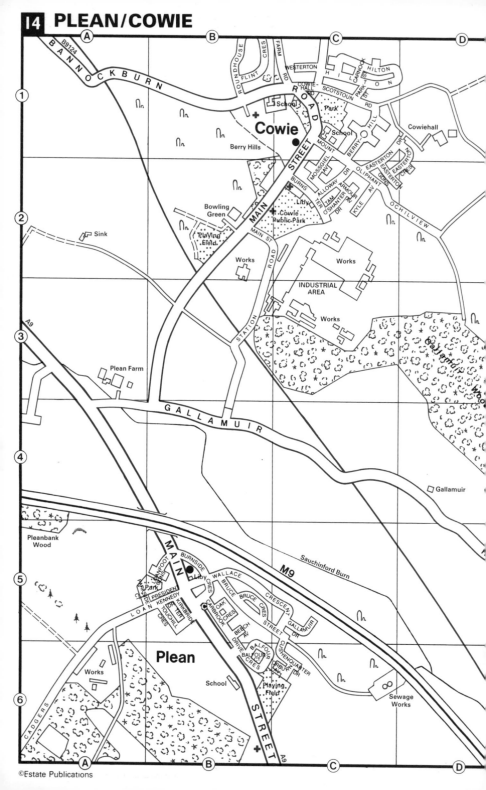

14 PLEAN/COWIE

Cowie

Plean

©Estate Publications

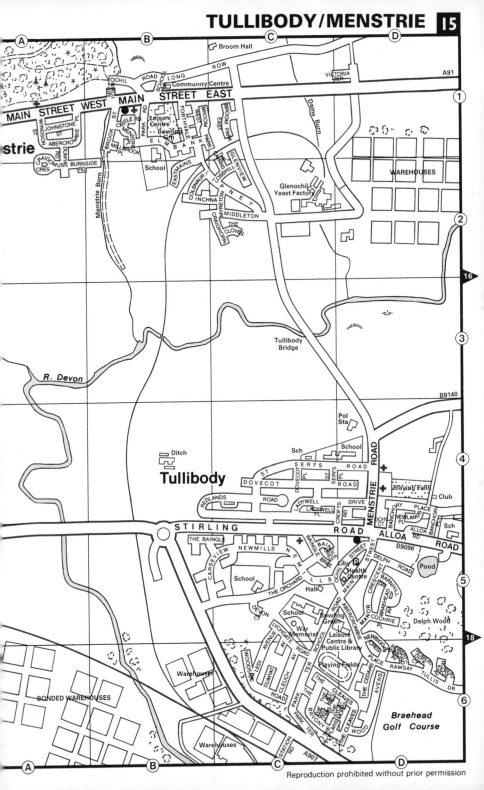

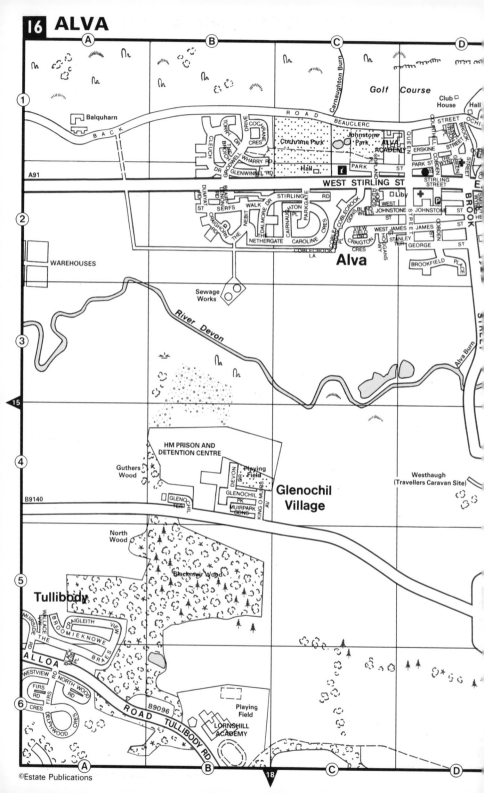

16 ALVA

Balquharn

Golf Course

Club House

Hall

BACK ROAD

A91

BEAUCLERC

OCHIL

COCHRANE CRES

TORRY DR

GROWNELL DR

CLEUCH

DRIVE

WHARRY RD

GLENWINNEL RD

Cochrane Park

Johnstone Park

ALVA ACADEMY

QUEEN ST

COURTHILL STREET

ERSKINE STREET

BRANK STREET

GREEN STREET

OCHIL STREET

PARK ST

COBDEN ST

Hall

WEST STIRLING ST

PARK ST

STIRLING STREET

DUNMAR ST

BRAE

SERFS

THE NEBIT

DALMORE DR

CRAIGHORN

CAIRNGORM

STIRLING PL

CAIRNAUGHTON CRES

PARKGATE

COBLECROOK PL

COBLECROOK PL

RD

i

Liby

WEST JOHNSTONE ST

WEST JAMES ST

JOHNSTONE ST

JAMES ST

WALK

NETHERGATE

CAROLINE

COBLECROOK LA

WEST STANLEY TERR

HOGANS

VIEW CRAIGTON CRES

GEORGE ST

STANLEY ST

Alva

BROOKFIELD PLACE

WAREHOUSES

EAST BROOK STREET

Sewage Works

River Devon

Alva Burn

15

HM PRISON AND DETENTION CENTRE

Guthers Wood

Playing Field

DEVON DR

GLENOCHIL PK

MUIRPARK GDNS

KING O MUIRS AV

Glenochil Village

Westhaugh (Travellers Caravan Site)

B9140

GLENOCHIL TER

North Wood

Blackmuir Wood

Tullibody

INGLEITH

VIEW

BROOMIEKNOWE

WALLACE

MUIRSIDE RD

THE BRAES

ALLOA

WESTVIEW

FIRS RD

NORTH WOOD RD

FIRS RD

BEECHWOOD CRES

CRES

ROAD

TULLIBODY RD

B9096

Playing Field

LORNSHILL ACADEMY

©Estate Publications

18

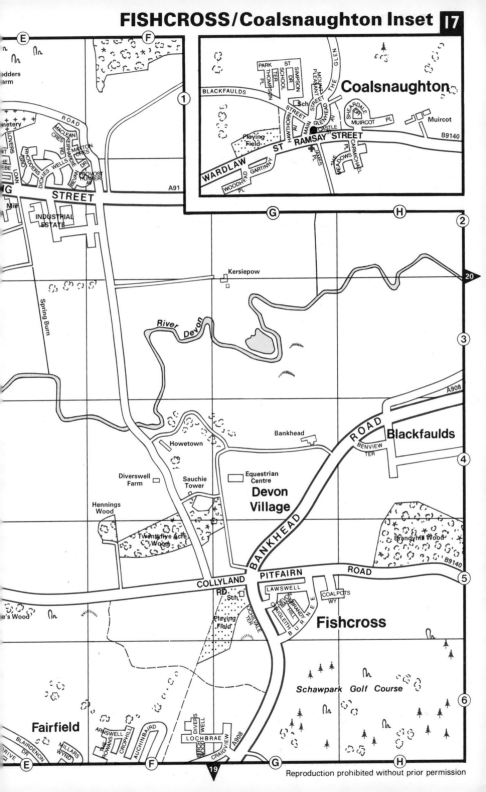

FISHCROSS/Coalsnaughton Inset

Coalsnaughton

PARK ST
SCHOOL
THOMSON TER
BLACKFAULDS
SIMPSON DR
PL
MOUNT PLEASANT
THE GLEN
Sch
MAIN STREET
STREET
GLENHEAD
CASTLE
SHEARDALE
MUIRCOT PL
Muircot
B9140
Playing Field
WARDLAW ST
RAMSAY STREET
JAMES PL
WOODHEAD PL
GARTINNY
PROVOST HUNTER AV
THE MEADOWS
CARMICHAEL

E
F
G
H

1
2
3
4
5
6

20
19

ROAD
MACLEAN CRES
MARTON CRES
WELLS AVE
DICKIES
MUIRHEAD RD
PROVOST HUNTER AV
LOVERS LOAN
RHODDERS GRO
Cemetery
STREET
A91
INDUSTRIAL ESTATE
Spring Burn
Mill

Kersiepow

River Devon

A908
ROAD
BENVIEW TER
Blackfaulds

Bankhead
Howetown
Diverswell Farm
Sauchie Tower
Equestrian Centre
Devon Village
Hennings Wood
Twentyfive Acre Wood

BANKHEAD
B9140
Brandyhill Wood

COLLYLAND RD.
PITFAIRN
LAWSWELL
DEVON PARK
CRAIGLEITH
HERALD MILL
BURNEE
COALPOTS WY
ROAD
Sch
LOCHVALE TER
Playing Field
Fishcross

's Wood

Schawpark Golf Course

Fairfield
ARNSWELL
ROWANS
CROPHILL
AUCHINBAIRD
DIVERS WELL
LOCHBRAE
CRAIGVIEW
A908
BLAIRDENON DRIVE
MILLARS WYND

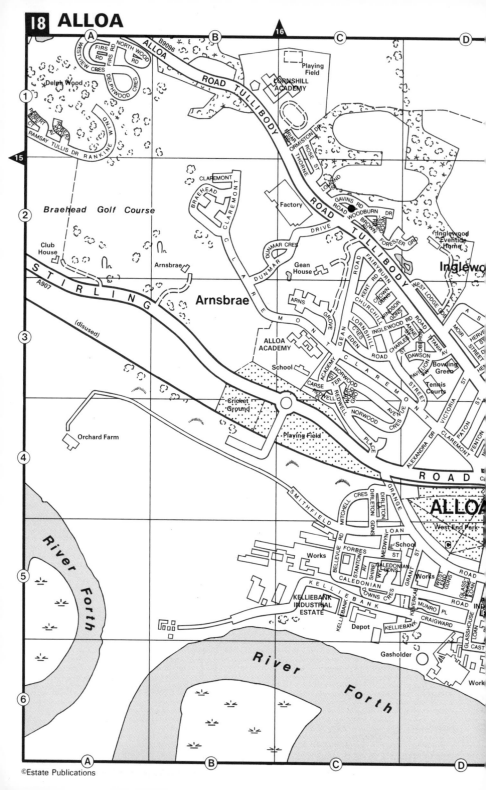

©Estate Publications

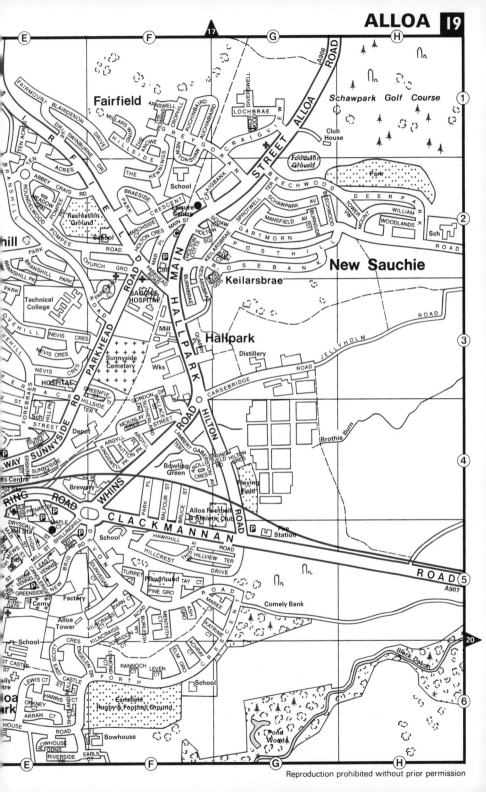

ALLOA 19

Reproduction prohibited without prior permission

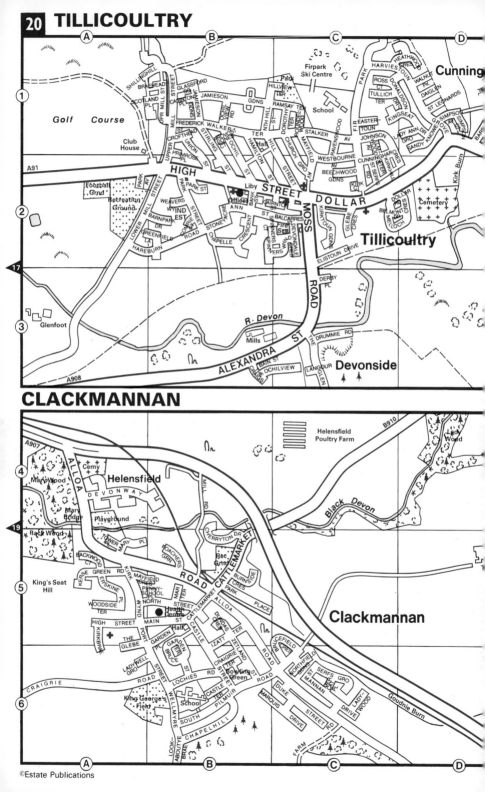

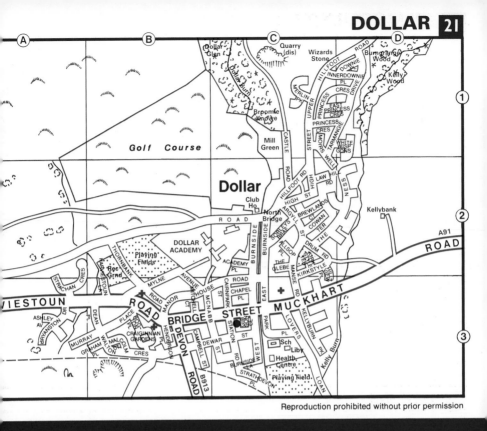

A - Z INDEX TO STREETS
with Postcodes

x includes some names ch there is insufficient on the maps. These are preceded by an * followed by the nearest g thoroughfare.

STIRLING

Mill. FK8	9 G5
Rd. FK8	9 F4
Rd Pl. FK8	9 F5
Vw. FK9	9 G1
d. FK7	11 G3
sford Pl,	
r Pl. FK8	9 F4
mby Dri. FK9	7 E3
mby Pl. FK8	3 B5
Av. FK9	9 G1
y Rd. FK8	13 C2
ra Pl. FK9	3 B4
Dri. FK9	9 E2
n Pl. FK9	9 E2
FK7	11 F2
. FK7	11 F3
. FK9	7 E5
Rd. FK9	7 F5
Cres. FK7	11 F6
l. FK8	3 A5
t. FK15	5 C5
er Dri. FK9	6 D3
ra Pl. FK9	9 F4
. FK8	3 C6
k. FK9	6 C3
ale Rd. FK9	6 D3
er Gdns. FK9	7 E3
t Ct. FK9	7 E3

Alloa Rd. FK9	9 G1
Alloway Dri. FK7	14 C2
Almond Ct. FK7	11 F2
Anchorscross. FK15	4 B4
Anderson Clo. FK7	10 D3
Anderson Ct. FK15	4 C4
Anderson St. FK15	4 C4
Anne Av. FK9	7 E4
Anne St. FK15	4 C4
Annfield Dri. FK7	11 F2
Annfield Gdns. FK8	11 E2
Annfield Gro. FK8	11 E2
Arbroath Cres. FK9	9 F1
Arcade. FK8	3 C5
Archers Av. FK7	11 G4
Ardoch Cres. FK15	4 C4
Argyle Gro. FK15	5 C5
Argyle Pk. FK15	5 B5
Argyle Ter. FK15	5 B5
Argyle Way. FK15	5 B5
Argyll Av. FK8	3 D2
Armour Av. FK7	14 C2
Ash Ter. FK8	10 C3
Ashbrae Gdns. FK7	11 E5
Atholl Ct. FK15	4 C4
Atholl Pl,	
Dunblane. FK15	4 C4
Atholl Pl, Stirling. FK8	8 C3
Auchinlay Rd. FK15	4 B3
Avenue Pk. FK9	6 D3
Back o' Dykes Rd. FK9	7 G4
Back o' Hill Rd. FK8	3 A5
Back o' Muir Rd. FK13	13 C3
Back Wk. FK8	3 B4
Backcroft. FK15	4 D3
Baillie Waugh Rd. FK7	11 F4
Baker St. FK8	3 B4
Balfour Ct. FK7	14 B6
Balfour Cres. FK7	14 B6

Balfour St,	
Bannockburn. FK7	13 A1
Balfour St, Stirling. FK8	8 C3
Ballater Dri. FK9	9 F1
Ballengeich Pass FK8	3 A2
Ballengeich Rd. FK8	3 A2
Balmoral Ct. FK15	5 C5
Balmoral Pl. FK8	3 A5
Balquhidderock. FK7	11 G4
Balure Cres. FK7	12 F2
Bandeath Rd. FK7	12 F3
Bank St. FK8	3 C4
Bannock Rd. FK7	12 E2
Bannockburn Rd,	
Cowie. FK7	14 A1
Bannockburn Rd,	
St Ninians. FK7	11 E4
Bannockburn	
Station Rd. FK7	12 C3
Barbour Av. FK7	11 G4
Barn Rd. FK8	3 B3
Barnsdale Rd. FK7	10 D5
Barnton St. FK8	3 C3
Barnwell Dri. FK9	9 F1
Barony Ct. FK7	10 A2
Batterflatts Gdns. FK7	10 C2
Baxter St. FK7	12 F3
Baxters Loan. FK15	5 A5
Bayne St. FK8	3 C2
Bearside Rd. FK7	10 D5
Beaton Av. FK7	13 A2
Beatty Av. FK8	8 D3
Beda Pl. FK7	12 E2
Beech Av. FK7	14 B5
Beech La. FK7	9 F1
Beech Rd. FK15	4 D4
Bellfield Rd,	
Bannockburn. FK7	13 C2

Bellfield Rd,	
St Ninians. FK8	11 E3
Bentheads. FK7	13 C2
Benview. FK7	11 F5
Berkeley St. FK7	10 D3
Berryhill. FK7	14 C1
Birch Av. FK8	10 C3
Birkhill Rd. FK7	10 B2
Bishops Gdns. FK15	4 C4
Blairforkie Dri. FK9	6 C2
Bogend Rd. FK7	13 C2
Bogside. FK15	4 D3
Bohun Ct. FK7	11 G4
Borestone Ct. FK7	11 E5
Borestone Cres. FK7	11 E4
Borestone Pl. FK7	11 E5
Borrowlea Rd. FK7	11 F1
Borrowmeadow Rd. FK7	9 G6
Braehead Rd. FK7	11 F5
Braemar Av. FK15	5 B5
Braemar Gro. FK15	5 B5
Braemar Pk. FK15	5 B5
Braeport. FK15	4 D4
Brentham Av. FK8	11 E2
Brentham Cres. FK8	11 E2
Bridge End. FK15	4 D4
Bridgehaugh Rd. FK9	9 E3
Broad St. FK8	3 B4
Broadleys Rd. FK9	9 G6
Brock Pl. FK7	11 F5
Broom Ct. FK7	11 F4
Broom Rd. FK7	11 F3
Broomhill Pl. FK7	10 B1
Broomridge Rd. FK7	11 F5
Brown Av. FK9	9 F3
Bruce Av. FK15	4 B4
Bruce Cres. FK7	14 B5
Bruce Dri. FK7	12 F2

Bruce St,	
Bannockburn. FK7	13 C1
Bruce St, Plean. FK7	14 B5
Bruce St, Stirling. FK8	3 C2
Bruce Ter. FK7	10 B2
Bruce Vw. FK7	11 E6
Buccleuth Ct. FK15	4 C3
Buchan Dri. FK15	4 B4
Buchanan Dri. FK9	9 F2
Buntine Cres. FK7	10 D4
Burghmuir Rd,	
St Ninians. FK7	11 E4
Burghmuir Rd,	
Stirling. FK8	3 C2
Burn Dri. FK7	11 F3
Burns St. FK8	9 E3
Burnside Cres. FK7	14 B5
Burnside St. FK7	11 F1
Cadgers Loan. FK7	14 A1
Cairnoch Way. FK7	13 D1
Calder Ct. FK7	11 F3
Caledonian Pl. FK15	4 C4
Calton Cres. FK7	11 E3
Caltrop Pl. FK7	11 H4
Cameronian St. FK8	3 D6
Campbell Ct. FK7	10 D4
Canavan Ct. FK7	11 F4
Carbrook Dri. FK7	14 B5
Carlie Av. FK9	7 E5
Carmichael Ct. FK9	7 E4
Carnock St. FK7	14 C1
Carrick Ct. FK15	11 F3
Carron Pl. FK7	11 E5
Carsaig Ct. FK9	6 D6
Carse of Lecropt Rd. FK9	6 A6
Carseview. FK7	13 D1
Castle Ct. FK8	3 B3
Castle Rd. FK9	9 F2
Castle Wynd. FK8	3 B3

Castlevale. FK9 — 8 D1
Castleview Dri. FK9 — 6 D4
Catherine St. FK7 — 13 B1
Cauldhame Cres. FK7 — 10 A2
Causewayhead Rd. FK8 — 3 C1
Cawder Gdns. FK9 — 6 C3
Cawder Rd. FK9 — 6 C4
Cawdor Cres. FK15 — 4 B4
Cecil St. FK7 — 11 F2
Cedar Av. FK8 — 10 C3
Centenary Wk. FK9 — 6 D5
Chalton Cr. FK9 — 7 F4
Chalton Rd. FK9 — 7 E3
*Charles Av,
Queens Av. FK9 — 7 E4
Charles Rodger Pl. FK9 — 7 E5
Charles St,
Dunblane. FK15 — 5 C5
Charles St,
St Ninians. FK8 — 10 D2
Charter St. FK7 — 11 E5
Chartershall Rd. FK7 — 10 D5
Chattan Av. FK9 — 9 E1
Chisholm Av,
Cornton. FK9 — 9 E2
Chisholm Av,
Dunblane. FK15 — 4 D3
Churchill Dri. FK9 — 6 D5
Claremont Dri. FK9 — 7 F3
Clarendon Pl,
Dunblane. FK15 — 5 C5
Clarendon Pl,
Stirling. FK8 — 3 B6
Clarendon Rd. FK8 — 3 B5
Clark St. FK7 — 11 E5
Claycrofts Pl. FK7 — 11 F1
Claymore Dri. FK7 — 11 G4
Cleuch Rd. FK9 — 9 F2
Clifford Rd. FK8 — 11 E2
Coal Wynd. FK7 — 13 C2
Coldstream Av. FK15 — 4 B4
Colliers Ct. FK7 — 12 F3
Colquhoun St. FK7 — 11 F1
Coney Pk. FK7 — 10 C1
Coneyhill Rd. FK9 — 7 E4
Constable Ct. FK7 — 11 F2
Coppermine Pth. FK9 — 7 E3
Corbiewood Dri. FK7 — 13 C3
Corn Exchange Rd. FK8 — 3 C5
Cornhill Cres. FK7 — 11 E4
Cornton Cres. FK9 — 6 D5
Cornton Rd,
Bridge of Allan. FK9 — 6 D4
Cornton Rd,
Cornton. FK9 — 9 E2
Cowane St. FK8 — 3 C2
Cowie Rd. FK7 — 13 D2
Cowiehall Rd. FK7 — 14 C1
Coxburn Brae. FK9 — 6 D1
Coxhill Rd. FK7 — 10 D4
Craig Ct. FK7 — 7 E5
Craig Cres. FK9 — 9 G2
Craig Leith Rd. FK7 — 11 G2
Craigend Rd. FK7 — 10 D4
Craigford Dri. FK7 — 13 C2
Craigforth Cres. FK8 — 8 C4
Craighall St. FK8 — 8 C3
Cringate Gdns. FK7 — 13 D2
Crofthead St. FK8 — 3 B3
Crofthead Rd. FK8 — 3 B3
Cromlix Cres. FK15 — 4 B4
Cruachan Av. FK9 — 9 E2
Crum Cres. FK7 — 11 F5
Cultenhove Cres. FK7 — 10 D4
Cultenhove Pl. FK7 — 10 D4
Cultenhove Rd. FK7 — 10 D4
Cunningham Rd. FK7 — 11 G1
Cushenquarter Dri. FK7 — 14 C6
Dalgleish Ct. FK8 — 3 C4
Dalmorglen Pk. FK7 — 10 C2
Dargai Ter. FK15 — 4 C3
Darn Rd,
Bridge of Allan. FK9 — 6 C2
Darn Rd,
Dunblane. FK15 — 5 D5
Darnley St. FK8 — 3 B4
Davidson St. FK7 — 13 A2
Dean Cres. FK8 — 3 D2
Dermoch Dri. FK15 — 4 B4
Deroran Pl. FK8 — 10 C2
Devlin Ct. FK7 — 11 E6
Donaldson Pl. FK7 — 10 B2
Douglas Dri. FK7 — 11 G4
Douglas St,
Bannockburn. FK7 — 13 C1
Douglas St, Stirling. FK8 — 3 C2
Douglas Ter. FK7 — 10 B1
Doune Rd. FK15 — 4 A3

Dowan Pl. FK7 — 10 B1
Downie Pl. FK7 — 13 C1
Drip Rd. FK8 — 3 B1
Drummond Pl. FK8 — 10 D1
Drummond Pl La. FK8 — 10 D1
Drummond Rise. FK15 — 4 D4
Drumpark St. FK7 — 11 E4
Duff Cres. FK8 — 8 C4
Duke St. FK7 — 11 F6
Dumbarton Rd. FK8 — 3 C5
Dumyat Rd. FK9 — 9 F2
Dundas Rd. FK9 — 9 E1
Dunster Rd. FK9 — 9 F2
Dunvegan Dri. FK9 — 9 F3
Dykedale. FK15 — 4 E4
Earlsburn Av. FK7 — 10 D4
Earlshill Dri. FK7 — 13 D1
East Murrayfield. FK7 — 13 C2
Easter Cornton Rd. FK9 — 9 E1
Easter Livilands. FK7 — 11 F3
Easterton Cres. FK7 — 14 C2
Easterton Dri. FK7 — 14 C2
Easterton Gdns. FK7 — 14 C2
Easton Ct. FK8 — 9 E3
Eccles Ct. FK7 — 11 E3
Edward Av. FK8 — 9 F4
Edward Pl. FK15 — 5 C5
Edward Rd. FK8 — 3 D2
Edward St. FK15 — 5 C5
Elgin Dri. FK7 — 11 F4
Elizabeth St. FK8 — 10 D2
Elm St. FK8 — 8 C4
Elmbank Rd. FK7 — 10 D5
Endrick Pl. FK7 — 10 D4
Etive Pl. FK9 — 9 E2
Ewing Ct. FK7 — 11 F4
Fairgreen Pl. FK7 — 13 D2
Fairhill Rd. FK7 — 11 E6
Farm St,
Bannockburn. FK7 — 13 C2
Farm Rd, Cowie. FK7 — 14 C1
Farm Rd, Fallin. FK7 — 12 F2
Ferguson St. FK8 — 8 D3
*Ferndene Ter,
New Rd. FK7 — 13 B1
Ferniebank Brae. FK9 — 6 C2
Ferry Orchard. FK9 — 9 G4
Ferry Rd. FK9 — 9 G4
Firpark Ter. FK7 — 10 A2
Firs Cres. FK7 — 11 G5
Firs Entry. FK7 — 11 G5
Fishers Grn. FK7 — 6 D1
Flint Cres. FK7 — 14 B1
Forglen Cres. FK9 — 7 E5
Forglen Rd. FK9 — 7 E5
Forrest Rd. FK8 — 3 D2
Forth Ct. FK8 — 3 D2
Forth Cres. FK8 — 3 D3
Forth Pl,
Bridge of Allan. FK9 — 6 D6
Forth Pl, Stirling. FK8 — 3 D3
Forth St, Fallin. FK7 — 12 E2
Forth St, Stirling. FK8 — 3 D2
Forthview,
Bannockburn. FK7 — 13 D1
Forthview, Stirling. FK8 — 3 D2
Fountain Rd. FK9 — 6 D4
Fraser Pl. FK9 — 9 E1
Friars St. FK8 — 3 C5
Gallamuir Dri. FK7 — 14 C5
Gallamuir Rd. FK7 — 14 B4
Gambeson Cres. FK7 — 11 G4
Gartclush Gdns. FK7 — 13 D2
Gateside Rd. FK7 — 10 D5
George St. FK15 — 5 C5
Gillespie Pl. FK7 — 11 F6
Gillies Dri. FK7 — 11 F3
Gillies Hill. FK7 — 10 A2
Gladstone Pl. FK8 — 11 E1
Glaive Av. FK7 — 11 G4
Glasgow Rd. FK7 — 11 E4
Glebe Av. FK8 — 3 B6
Glebe Cres. FK8 — 3 B6
Glebe Pl. FK15 — 4 C4
Glen Ct. FK15 — 4 E4
Glen Rd,
Bridge of Allan. FK9 — 6 D2
Glen Rd,
Dunblane. FK15 — 4 D4
Glen Tye Rd. FK7 — 12 G2
Glenallan Ct. FK15 — 5 C5
Glencairn St. FK7 — 11 F4
Glencoe Rd. FK8 — 3 B2
Glendevon Dri. FK8 — 3 A1
Gogar Pl. FK7 — 11 F5
Goosecroft Rd. FK8 — 3 C3
Gordon Cres,
Bridge of Allan. FK9 — 6 D3

Gordon Cres,
Stirling. FK8 — 8 C3
Gowanhill Gdns. FK8 — 3 A1
Gracie Cres. FK7 — 12 F3
Graham Av. FK9 — 9 G1
Graham St. FK9 — 7 E4
Grampian Rd. FK9 — 10 B2
Grange Gdns. FK9 — 7 F4
Grant Dri. FK15 — 4 B3
Grant Pl. FK9 — 9 E2
Graystale Rd. FK9 — 10 D5
Greenacre Ct. FK7 — 13 C2
Greenacre Pl. FK7 — 13 C2
Greenwood Av. FK8 — 3 A4
Grendon Ct. FK8 — 11 E2
Grendon Gdns. FK8 — 10 D2
Grierson Cres. FK7 — 10 A2
Haig Av. FK8 — 9 E3
Haining. FK15 — 4 C3
Halberts Cres. FK7 — 11 E5
Haldane Av. FK9 — 7 E5
Hamilton Dri. FK9 — 9 F1
Hanover Ct,
Causewayhead. FK9 — 9 G1
Hanover Ct,
Dunblane. FK15 — 5 C5
Hardie Ct. FK7 — 11 F4
Hardie Cres. FK7 — 12 E2
Hart Wynd. FK7 — 13 D2
Harvey Wynd. FK8 — 3 B2
Haugh Rd. FK9 — 9 E3
Hawthorn Cres,
Fallin. FK7 — 12 F3
Hawthorn Cres,
Stirling. FK8 — 8 D3
Hawthorn Dri. FK7 — 12 E2
Hayford Pl. FK7 — 10 B2
Hazelbank Gdns. FK8 — 8 D3
Hedges Loan. FK7 — 13 C2
Henderson St. FK9 — 6 D3
Henry Milne Wk. FK7 — 7 H5
Hermitage Rd. FK9 — 7 G5
High St. FK15 — 4 D4
Highfields. FK15 — 5 B5
Hill St. FK7 — 11 E4
Hillfoots Rd. FK9 — 9 G1
Hillpark Cres. FK7 — 13 B1
Hillpark Dri. FK7 — 13 B1
Hillside Av. FK15 — 5 C5
Hillview Dri. FK7 — 7 E4
Hillview Pl. FK7 — 12 E2
Hilton. FK7 — 14 C1
Hilton Ter. FK7 — 12 E3
Hirst Ct. FK7 — 12 F3
Hirst Cres. FK7 — 12 F3
Holme Hill Ct. FK15 — 4 D4
Hope St. FK8 — 8 C4
Hopetoun Dri. FK9 — 6 D3
Howlands Rd. FK7 — 10 D5
Hume Ct. FK9 — 7 E5
Hume Cres. FK9 — 6 D5
Huntley Cres. FK8 — 8 C3
INDUSTRIAL ESTATES:
Back o'Hill Ind Est. FK8 — 3 A1
Broadleys Ind Pk. FK7 — 11 G2
Castle Business Pk. FK8 — 3 A1
Dockburn Ind Est. FK15 — 5 C5
Springkerse
Ind Est. FK7 — 11 G1
Stirling Enterprise Pk.
FK7 — 11 F2
Thistle Ind Est. FK7 — 11 F1
Inverallan Ct. FK9 — 6 C3
Inverallan Dri. FK9 — 6 C4
Inverallan Rd. FK9 — 6 C4
Irvine Pl. FK8 — 3 B3
Ivanhoe Pl. FK8 — 8 D3
Jail Wynd. FK8 — 3 B4
James St,
Bannockburn. FK7 — 13 B2
James St, Stirling. FK8 — 3 D2
John Murray Dri. FK9 — 6 D3
John R. Gray Rd. FK15 — 5 C5
Johnson Av. FK9 — 9 E2
Johnston St. FK7 — 13 A1
Keir Av. FK8 — 9 E3
Keir Ct. FK9 — 7 E4
Keir Gdns. FK9 — 6 D4
Keir La. FK15 — 5 E5
Keir St,
Bridge of Allan. FK9 — 6 D4
Keir St, Dunblane. FK15 — 4 C4
Keith Av. FK7 — 11 F4
Kelly Ct. FK8 — 3 B4
Kenilworth Ct. FK9 — 7 F4
Kenilworth Rd. FK9 — 7 E3
Kenningknowes Rd. FK8 — 10 C2
Kent Rd. FK7 — 11 F2

Kerse Rd. FK7 — 11 F1
Kersebonny Rd. FK7 — 10 A1
Kilbryde Ct. FK15 — 4 C4
Kilbryde Cres. FK15 — 4 B3
Kilbryde Gro. FK15 — 4 C3
King St, Fallin. FK7 — 12 E2
King St, Stirling. FK8 — 3 C5
Kings Park Rd. FK8 — 3 B6
Kingstables La. FK8 — 3 B3
Kinnoull Av. FK15 — 4 B4
Kippendavie Av. FK15 — 4 E2
Kippendavie La. FK15 — 4 E2
Kippendavie Rd. FK15 — 4 E2
Kirk St. FK15 — 4 D4
Kirk Wynd. FK7 — 11 E3
Kirkbridge Ter. FK7 — 14 B5
Kyle Av. FK7 — 14 C2
Laburnum Gro. FK8 — 10 D2
Lademill. FK7 — 13 A2
Ladysneuk Rd. FK9 — 9 G2
Laighhill Ct. FK15 — 4 D3
Laighhill Pl. FK15 — 4 D3
Lamberton Av. FK7 — 11 F4
Lamont Cres. FK7 — 12 F2
Landrick Av. FK15 — 4 E2
Laurelhill Gdns. FK8 — 10 D2
Laurelhill Pl. FK8 — 10 D2
Laurencecroft Rd. FK8 — 3 C1
Ledi Vw. FK9 — 9 E2
Leewood Pk. FK15 — 5 E5
Leewood Rd. FK15 — 5 E5
Leighton Av. FK15 — 4 F4
Leighton Ct. FK15 — 4 F4
Lennox Av. FK7 — 11 E3
Linden Av. FK7 — 11 F1
Lindsay Dri. FK9 — 9 E1
Lister Ct. FK9 — 6 D5
Livilands Ct. FK8 — 11 E2
Livilands Gate. FK8 — 11 E2
Livilands La. FK8 — 11 E2
Loanfoot Gdns. FK7 — 14 B5
Logie La. FK9 — 7 F4
Logie Rd. FK9 — 9 G1
Lomond Cres. FK9 — 9 E1
Lomond Dri. FK7 — 13 C1
Lothian Cres. FK9 — 9 F1
Lovers Walk. FK8 — 3 C1
Lower Bridge St. FK8 — 3 C1
Lower Castlehill. FK8 — 3 B3
Lyon Cres. FK9 — 6 D4
McAlley Ct. FK9 — 6 D4
McAllister Ct. FK7 — 13 C1
Macdonald Dri. FK7 — 10 D4
McGrigor Rd. FK7 — 11 E4
McLachlan Av. FK7 — 11 E5
McLaren Ter. FK7 — 11 E5
McPherson Dri. FK8 — 8 D3
Mace Ct. FK7 — 11 H4
Main St,
Cambusbarron. FK7 — 10 A2
Main St,
Bannockburn. FK7 — 13 C1
Main St, Plean. FK7 — 14 B2
Main St, St Ninians. FK7 — 11 E4
Maitland Av. FK7 — 13 C2
Maitland Cres. FK7 — 11 E5
Manse Cres. FK7 — 11 E3
Manse Pl. FK7 — 13 D1
Mar Pl. FK8 — 3 B3
Margaret Rd. FK7 — 11 F6
Marlborough Dri. FK9 — 9 F2
Marschall Ct. FK7 — 11 G4
Maurice Av. FK7 — 11 G3
Maxwell Pl. FK8 — 3 C4
Mayfield Ct. FK7 — 11 E4
Mayfield St. FK7 — 11 E4
Mayne Av. FK9 — 7 E4
Meadow Pl. FK8 — 9 F4
Meadowforth Rd. FK7 — 11 F1
Meadowland Rd. FK7 — 7 E4
Melfort Dri. FK7 — 11 F3
Melville Pl. FK9 — 7 E4
Melville Ter. FK8 — 3 C6
Mentieth Rd. FK9 — 9 E2
Mentieth Vw. FK7 — 14 E3
Menzies Dri. FK7 — 8 D3
Middlemuir Rd. FK7 — 11 F1
Mill Ct. FK15 — 4 C3
Mill Rd. FK7 — 10 A1
Mill Row. FK15 — 4 C4
Millar Pl. FK8 — 9 F4
Millhall Rd. FK7 — 11 G3
Millhill. FK7 — 10 A2
Milnepark Rd. FK7 — 13 C2
Milton. FK7 — 13 A2
Milton Brae. FK7 — 11 E5
Milton Cres. FK7 — 13 A1

Milton Gdns. FK7
Milton Rd. FK7
Milton Ter. FK7
Mine Rd. FK9
Modan Rd. FK7
Montgomery Way. FK
Montrose Rd. FK9
Montrose Way. FK15
Morgan Ct. FK7
Morley Cres. FK7
Morris Ter. FK8
Morrison Dri. FK7
Moss Rd. FK7
Mossgiel Av.
Cowie. FK7
Mossgiel Av,
Stirling. FK8
Mount Oliphant. FK7
Mowbray Ct. FK7
Muiralehouse Rd. FK7
Muirend Rd. FK8
Muirton Rd. FK7
Munro Av. FK9
Munro Rd. FK7
Murdoch Ter. FK15
Murnin Ct. FK7
Murray Pl,
Cambusbarron. FK7
Murray Pl, Stirling. FK
Murrayfield Pl. FK7
Murrayfield Ter. FK7
Murrayshall Rd. FK7
Myreton Dri. FK7
Nailer Rd. FK7
Nelson Pl. FK7
New Line Rd. FK7
New Rd. FK7
New St. FK9
Newhouse. FK8
Newlands Rd. FK7
Newmarket. FK7
Newpark Cres. FK7
Newpark Rd. FK7
Newton Cres. FK15
Newton Loan. FK15
North End Rd. FK7
North St. FK9
Oak Cres. FK7
Oak Dri. FK7
Oak St. FK8
Ochil Cres. FK8
Ochil Rd. FK9
Ochil St. FK7
Ochilmount. FK7
Ochiltree. FK15
Ochiltree Ct. FK15
Ochilview. FK7
Ochlochy Pk. FK15
Ogilvie Pl. FK7
Ogilvie Rd. FK8
Old Doune Rd. FK15
Old Drove Rd. FK7
Old Military Rd. FK9
Orchard Rd. FK7
Park Av. FK8
Park Cres. FK7
Park Dri. FK7
Park Gdns. FK7
Park La. FK8
Park Pl. FK7
Park St. FK7
Park Ter. FK8
Parkdyke. FK7
Parkside Ct. FK7
Paterson Pl. FK9
Pathfoot Av. FK9
Pathfoot Dri. FK9
Pelstream Av. FK7
Pendreich Rd. FK9
Pendreich Way. FK9
Perth Rd. FK15
Peterswell Brae. FK7
Pike Rd. FK7
Pirnhall Rd. FK7
Pitt Ter. FK8
Polmaise Av. FK7
Polmaise Cres. FK7
Polmaise Rd. FK7
Port St. FK8
Pottis Rd. FK7
President Kennedy Dri.
FK7
Princes St. FK8
Pullar Av. FK9
Pullar Ct. FK9
Quakerfield. FK7
Quarry Knowe. FK7

id. FK7　10 A2
t.
ckburn. FK7　11 F6
t, Fallin. FK7　12 E3
t, Stirling. FK8　3 C3
Av. FK9　7 E4
i Ct.
ns La. FK9　6 D3
La. FK9　6 D3
Rd. FK8　3 A5
augh Dri. FK8　9 F4
Pl. FK8　3 B1
h Ct. FK8　11 E2
h Cres. FK7　13 A1
h Pl. FK7　13 B1
h Rd. FK8　11 E3
h Ter. FK7　11 E3
Rd. FK8　8 C3
ie. FK15　4 D3
t. FK15　4 C4
ik Vw. FK8　9 F5
e Dri. FK8　9 G4
on Pl. FK7　11 E4
Way. FK15　5 B5
Pl. FK8　3 D3
y Pl. FK8　3 D3
y Ter. FK8　3 D3
FK7　11 F4
use. FK7　14 B1
urn Rd. FK9　7 E5
n Dri. FK7　13 D2
Ct. FK7　13 C2
dns. FK8　3 A4
The Path. FK7　13 B1
The Yetts. FK7　10 A2
Thistle Shopping
　Centre. FK8　3 D5
Thomson Ct. FK7　10 D3
Torbrex. FK7　10 D3
s Rd. FK15　4 D4
ent Av. FK15　5 B5
s Cres. FK9　9 G4
s Orch. FK9　9 G5
St. FK8　3 B4
nce Av. FK15　5 B5
arets Dri. FK15　4 E4
arets Loan. FK15　4 E4
s Ct. FK15　4 D4
s Dri. FK15　4 D4
s Wynd. FK8　3 B3
ns Rd,
usbarron. FK7　10 B2
ns Rd,
g.　3 C6
has's Pl. FK7　10 B1
has's Well. FK7　10 B1
y Ct. FK7　10 D3
y Dri. FK7　10 D3
Ct. FK7　13 D2
St. FK7　10 D5
n Way. FK7　11 G4
un Rd. FK7　14 C1
i. FK15　4 B4
. FK8　9 E3
i Pl. FK8　3 C4
ri. FK7　11 F4
ri Rd. FK9　9 F4
Brae Rd. FK7　11 E3
d. FK8　3 D4
Ct. FK7　13 D1
Dri. FK7　12 F3
s St. FK15　4 D4
Loan. FK15　4 D4
n Pl. FK7　10 D1
n Pl La. FK8　10 D2
.t. FK9　9 G4
eld Cres. FK8　10 D1
, FK7　11 F3
ill. FK9　7 G6
st. FK8　3 B4
ank Cres. FK15　4 B3
ank Gdns. FK15　4 B3
ank Rd. FK7　11 F1
eld Ct. FK15　4 C4
eld Dri. FK7　11 F2
eld Ter. FK15　4 C4
erse Rd. FK7　11 F1
vood Av. FK7　10 C2
Dri. FK7　7 E4
Rd,
ockburn. FK7　13 C1
Rd,
e of Allan. FK9　6 C3
Rd, Cowie. FK7　14 B3
Rd,
ane. FK15　4 C4
Rd, Stirling. FK8　3 C5
i. FK7　13 D2

Stevenson Ct. FK9　7 E5
Stewart Rd. FK9　6 C4
Stewart Sq. FK8　8 D3
Stewart St. FK7　10 B1
Stirling Rd. FK15　5 C5
Stirling Rd. FK7　12 D2
Strathallan Ct. FK9　6 D5
Strathallan Rd. FK9　6 D4
Strathmore Av. FK15　4 B3
Strathmore Cres. FK9　9 E2
Strathmore Dri. FK9　9 E2
Sunnybank Rd. FK7　11 E4
Sunnylaw Rd. FK9　6 D2
Sunnylaw Rd. FK9　7 E3
Sunnyside. FK7　11 E4
Surcoat Loan. FK7　11 H4
Sutherland Ter. FK9　9 F4
Sycamore Pl. FK8　10 C3
Symon Field. FK15　4 D4
Tam o'Shanter Dri. FK7　14 C2
Tannahill Ter. FK15　4 C3
Tannery La. FK7　13 C1
Telford Ct. FK7　13 C1
The Avenue. FK9　6 D3
The Brae,
　Bannockburn. FK7　13 C1
The Brae,
　Cambusbarron. FK7　10 A2
The Crescent. FK15　4 D4
The Cross. FK15　4 C4
The Firs. FK7　11 G5
The Homesteads. FK7　10 B1

Union St. FK8　3 C2
Upper Bridge St. FK8　3 B3
Upper Castlehill. FK8　3 B3
Upper Craigs. FK8　3 C6
Upper Glen Rd. FK9　6 D2
Vale Gro. FK8　6 D6
Valleyfield Pl. FK7　11 F1
Victoria Pl. FK8　3 A6
Victoria Rd. FK8　3 B5
Victoria Sq. FK8　3 A5
Viewfield St. FK8　3 C4
Voil Rd. FK9　9 E2
Vorlich Pl. FK9　9 E2
Wallace Cres. FK7　14 B5
Wallace Gdns. FK9　9 G2
Wallace Pl,
　Cambusbarron. FK7　10 B3
Wallace Pl, Fallin. FK7　12 E2
Wallace Rd. FK15　4 B4
Wallace St,
　Bannockburn. FK7　13 D2
Wallace St, Stirling. FK8　3 C3
Wallstale Rd. FK7　10 D4
Waverley Cres. FK8　9 F4
Weaver Row. FK7　11 E3
Weir Dri. FK7　12 F3
Well Pl. FK15　4 C4
Well Rd. FK9　6 D3
Wellgate St. FK7　7 F4
Wellgreen. FK8　3 C6
Wellgreen Rd. FK8　3 C6
Wellpark Cres. FK7　10 D3
Welsh Gdns. FK8　6 D3
West Murrayfield. FK7　13 C2
Westerlands Dri. FK8　11 E3
Westerlea Dri. FK8　6 D6
Westerlea Pl. FK9　14 C1
Westerton. FK7　6 D4
Westerton Dri. FK7　6 D4
Whins Rd. FK7　11 F5
Whinwell Rd. FK8　3 B3
Whitecross Av. FK15　4 E2
Whitehill St. FK8　8 C3
Whitehouse St. FK11　11 G1
Wier St. FK8　8 C3
Willam Booth Pl. FK7　10 D4
Williamfield Av. FK7　11 E3
Wilson Dri. FK8　13 B1
Windsor Pl. FK8　3 B6
Wishart Dri. FK7　11 G4
Woodside Ct. FK7　10 A2
Woodside Pl. FK7　12 E2

Woodside Rd. FK8　8 D3

ALLOA

Abbey Craig Rd. FK10　19 E2
Abercrombie Pl,
　Menstrie. FK11　15 A1
Abercrombie Pl,
　Tullibody. FK10　15 D5
Academy Pl. FK14　21 C2
Academy St. FK10　18 C3
Achray Ct. FK10　19 F6
Alexandra Dri. FK10　18 D4
Alexandra St. FK13　20 B3
Alloa Rd,
　Clackmannan. FK10　20 A4
Alloa Rd,
　New Sauchie. FK10　19 G1
Alloa Rd,
　Tullibody. FK10　15 D5
Allsop Pl. FK10　21 C2
Ann St. FK13　20 B2
Anne St. FK10　18 D3
Argyll Pl. FK10　19 F4
Argyll St, Alloa. FK10　19 F4
Argyll St, Dollar. FK14　21 C2
Arns Gro. FK10　18 C3
Arnswell. FK10　19 F1
Aroll Cres. FK10　19 E6
Arran Ct. FK10　19 E6
*Arthur Bett Ct,
　High St. FK13　20 C2
Ash Gro. FK10　19 F5
Ashley Av. FK14　21 A3
Ashley Ter. FK10　18 D3
Auchinbaird. FK10　19 F1
Back Rd, Alva. FK12　16 A1
Back Rd, Dollar. FK14　21 A3
Backwood Ct. FK10　20 A5
Bain St. FK13　20 B3
Baingle Brae. FK10　15 C5
Baingle Cres. FK10　15 C5
Balcarres St. FK13　20 C2
Balfour St. FK10　19 F4
Banchory Pl. FK10　15 D5
Bank St, Alloa. FK10　19 E5
Bank St,
　Tillicoultry. FK13　20 B2
Bards Way. FK10　20 D1
Barnhill Dri. FK10　15 D5
Barnpark Dri. FK13　20 B2
Beauclerc St. FK12　16 C1
Bedford Ct. FK10　18 D5
Bedford Pl. FK10　18 D5
Beechwood. FK10　19 G2
Beechwood Gdns.
　FK13　20 C2
Bellevue Rd. FK13　18 C5
Belmont Dri. FK13　20 C2
Benview Ter. FK10　17 H4
Bevan Ct. FK10　17 E2
Birchwood. FK10　19 G1
Blackfaulds St. FK13　Inset 17
Blackmuir Rd. FK10　16 A6
Blairdenon Rd. FK12　16 B2
Blairdenon Dri. FK10　19 E1
Blindwells. FK12　16 C2
Bogton Pl. FK14　21 B3
Bowhouse Gdns. FK10　19 E6
Bowhouse Rd. FK10　19 E6
Braehead, Alva. FK12　16 D1
Braehead,
　Arnsbrae. FK10　18 B2
Braehead,
　Tillicoultry. FK13　20 B1
Braehead Av. FK10　15 D5
Braeside. FK10　19 F2
Brandy Hill. FK10　17 G5
Branshill Pk. FK10　19 E2
Branshill Rd. FK10　19 E2
Brewlands Rd. FK14　21 C2
Briar Rd. FK10　18 C1
Bridge St. FK14　21 B3
*Bridge Ter,
　Shillinghill. FK10　19 E5
Broad St. FK10　19 E6
Brook St, Alva. FK10　16 D2
Brook St,
　Menstrie. FK11　15 B1
Brookfield Pl. FK12　16 D2
Broom Pk East. FK11　15 C1
Broom Pk West. FK11　15 B1
Broomieknowe. FK10　16 A5
Brown Av. FK10　18 C2
Bruce St, Alloa. FK10　19 F4
Bruce St,
　Clackmannan. FK10　20 B6

Brucefield Cres. FK10　20 C6
Bryanston Dri. FK14　21 A3
Burgh Mews. FK10　19 E5
Burleigh Way. FK10　19 F5
Burnbrae. FK10　19 F3
Burnbrae Gdns. FK12　16 D2
Burnee. FK10　17 G5
Burnside Cres. FK10　20 B5
Burnside La. FK14　21 C3
Burnside Rd. FK11　15 A1
Burnside St. FK10　19 G2
Cairnaughton Pl. FK12　16 C2
Cairnpark St. FK14　21 C3
Cairnton Pl. FK13　20 B1
Cairnton St. FK13　20 B3
Caledonian Gdns. FK10　18 C5
Caledonian Rd. FK10　18 C5
Campbell St. FK14　21 B3
Candleriggs. FK10　19 E5
*Candleriggs Ct,
　Candleriggs. FK10　19 E5
Carmichael Pl. FK13　Inset 17
Caroline Cres. FK12　16 C2
Carse Ter. FK10　18 C3
Carsebridge Rd. FK10　19 F3
Carseview. FK10　15 B5
*Castle Ct,
　Castle Rd. FK11　15 B1
Castle Rd,
　Menstrie. FK11　15 B1
Castle Rd, Dollar. FK14　21 C2
Castle St, Alloa. FK10　18 D6
Castle St,
　Clackmannan. FK10　20 B5
Castle St,
　Coalsnaughton. FK13　Inset 17
Castle Ter. FK10　20 B6
Cattlemarket. FK10　20 B5
Chalmers Pl. FK13　20 D1
Chapel Pl. FK14　21 C3
Chapelhill. FK10　20 B6
Chapelle Cres. FK13　20 B2
Charles St. FK10　18 C3
Charlotte Pl. FK13　20 D1
Cherryton Dri. FK10　20 B5
Church Gro,
　Alloa. FK10　19 E2
Church Gro,
　Tillicoultry. FK13　20 C1
Church St. FK10　19 E5
Churchill St. FK10　18 C3
Clackmannan Rd. FK10　19 F4
Claremont, Alloa. FK10　18 D4
Claremont,
　Arnsbrae. FK10　18 B2
Cleuch Av. FK10　15 C6
Cleuch Dri. FK12　16 B1
Coalgate. FK10　19 E5
Coalpots Way. FK10　17 G5
Cobden St. FK10　16 D1
Cobden St. FK12　16 D1
Coblecrook Gdns. FK12　16 C2
Coblecrook La. FK12　16 C2
Coblecrook Pl. FK12　16 C2
Cochrane Cres. FK12　16 B1
Cochrie Pl. FK10　15 D5
*Colliers Ct,
　Balcarres St. FK13　20 C2
Collyland Rd. FK10　17 F5
Colsnaur. FK11　15 B2
Comrie Ct. FK13　20 B2
Coningsby Pl. FK10　18 D5
Copland Pl. FK12　16 C2
Courthill. FK12　16 D1
Cowan Ter. FK14　21 C2
Craigbank. FK10　19 F2
Craigburn. FK11　15 C2
Craighorn Rd. FK12　16 B2
Craiginnian Gdns. FK14　21 B3
Craigleith. FK10　17 G5
Craigleith Vw. FK10　16 A5
Craigomus Cres. FK11　15 A1
Craigrie Rd. FK10　20 A6
Craigrie Ter. FK10　20 B6
Craigton Cres. FK12　16 C2
Craigview. FK10　19 G1
Craigward. FK10　18 D5
Crofthead. FK13　20 B1
Crofts Rd. FK13　15 D4
Croftshaw Rd. FK12　16 D2
Crophill. FK10　19 F1
Crown Gdns. FK10　18 C3
Cunningham Dri. FK10　20 C2
*Curran Ct,
　Stirling St. FK13　20 B1
Daiglen. FK13　20 D1
Dalmore Dri. FK12　16 B2
Dawson Av. FK10　18 D3
Dean Pl. FK14　21 B3

Deerpark. FK10　19 H2
Delph Rd. FK10　15 D5
Delphwood Cres. FK10　16 A6
Derby Pl. FK13　20 C3
Devon Bank. FK10　17 G5
Devon Ct. FK10　15 C5
Devon Dri. FK10　16 B4
Devon Rd, Alloa. FK10　19 F5
Devon Rd, Dollar. FK14　21 B3
Devondale Cres. FK13　20 C2
Devonway. FK10　20 A4
Dewar St. FK14　21 B3
Dickies Wells. FK12　17 E2
Dirleton Gdns. FK10　18 C4
Dirleton La. FK10　18 C4
Diverswell. FK10　19 G1
Dollar Rd. FK13　20 C2
Donaldson Dri. FK13　20 C1
Doo'Cot Brae. FK10　18 D3
Dorothy Ter. FK13　20 C1
Dovecot Pl. FK10　15 C4
Dovecot Rd. FK10　15 C4
Dovehill. FK10　19 E3
Downie Pl. FK14　21 D1
Downs Cres. FK10　18 C5
Drum Rd. FK14　21 C2
Drummie Rd. FK13　20 C3
Drysdale St. FK10　19 E5
Duke St. FK10　20 C6
*Duke St,
　Beauclerc St. FK12　16 D1
Dumyat Av. FK10　15 C6
Dumyat Av, Alva. FK12　16 B2
Dumyat Rd,
　Menstrie. FK11　15 A1
Duncanson Av. FK10　18 D3
Dundas Cres. FK10　20 B5
Dunmar Cres. FK10　18 B2
Dunmar Rd. FK10　18 B2
Dunvegan Ct. FK10　19 F5
Earl of Mar Ct. FK10　19 E3
Earls Ct. FK10　19 E6
Earn Ct. FK10　19 F5
East Burnside. FK14　21 C3
East Castle St. FK10　19 E6
East Mains. FK11　15 B2
East Princess Cres. FK14　21 C1
East Stirling St. FK12　16 D2
East Vennel. FK10　19 E5
Eastertoun. FK13　20 C1
Eden Rd. FK10　18 C3
Elistoun Dri. FK13　20 C2
Elm Gro. FK10　19 F6
Elmbank. FK11　15 B1
Elmwood Av. FK13　20 C1
Engelen Dri. FK10　19 E6
Erskine Pl. FK10　20 A5
Erskine St, Alloa. FK10　19 E4
Erskine St, Alva. FK12　16 D1
Fairfield. FK10　19 E1
Fairmount Dri. FK10　19 E1
Fairyburn Rd. FK10　18 C2
Farm Rd. FK10　20 C6
Fenton St. FK10　18 D4
Fir Park. FK13　20 C1
Firs Rd. FK10　16 A6
Forbes St. FK10　18 C5
Forebraes. FK10　19 E4
Forester Gro. FK10　18 C2
Forth Cres. FK10　19 F6
Forthvale. FK11　15 B1
Frederick St. FK13　20 B1
Gaberston Av. FK10　19 F4
Garden Pl. FK10　20 B5
Garden Ter. FK10　20 B6
Gartinny. FK13　Inset 17
Gartmorn Rd. FK10　19 G2
Garvally Cres. FK10　18 D3
Gavins Rd. FK10　18 C2
Gean Rd. FK10　18 C3
George St. FK12　16 D2
Gibson Clo. FK14　21 C3
Glassford Sq. FK13　20 B1
Glasshouse Loan. FK10　18 D5
Glebe Cres, Alva. FK12　17 E1
Glebe Cres,
　Tillicoultry. FK13　20 C2
Glebe Ter. FK10　19 E5
Glen View. FK12　16 D1
Glenhead Av. FK13　Inset 17
Glenochil Av. FK10　16 B4
Glenochil Ter. FK10　16 B4
Glenview. FK11　15 C2
Glenwinnel Rd. FK12　16 B2
Gordon Dri. FK10　19 F3
Graham Pl. FK14　21 B3
Grange Rd. FK10　18 C4
Grant St. FK10　18 D5
Greenfield La. FK13　20 B2

Street	Postcode	Grid Ref
Greenfield St.	FK10	19 F3
Greenhead.	FK12	16 D2
Greenside St.	FK10	19 E5
Greygoran.	FK10	19 F1
Grodwell Dri.	FK12	16 B2
Hallpark.	FK10	19 F3
Hamilton St.	FK13	20 B1
Hareburn Rd.	FK13	20 A2
Harris Ct.	FK10	19 E6
Harviestoun Av.	FK10	20 C1
Harviestoun La.	FK14	21 B3
Harviestoun Rd.	FK14	21 A3
Hawkhill Rd.	FK10	19 F5
Hawthorn Av.	FK13	Inset 17
Heathwood Cres.	FK13	20 D1
Henderson Av.	FK10	18 D3
Henderson Pl, Alva.	FK12	16 D1
Henderson Pl, Dollar.	FK14	21 B3
Henry St.	FK12	16 D2
Hervey St.	FK10	18 D3
High St, Alloa.	FK10	19 E5
High St, Clackmannan.	FK10	20 A5
High St, Dollar.	FK14	21 C2
High St, Tillicoultry.	FK13	20 B2
Hill Pk.	FK10	19 E4
Hill Pl.	FK10	19 E3
Hill St, Alloa.	FK10	19 E4
Hill St, Tillicoultry.	FK13	20 B1
Hillcrest Dri.	FK10	19 F5
Hillfoot Rd.	FK14	21 C2
Hillside.	FK10	19 F1
Hillside Ter.	FK10	19 E4
Hillview Pl.	FK14	21 C2
Hillview Rd, Alloa.	FK10	19 F5
Hillview Ter, Tillicoultry.	FK13	20 B1
Hilton Cres.	FK10	19 G4
Hilton Rd.	FK10	19 F4
Hoggans Way.	FK12	16 C2
*Holbourne Pl, Main St East.	FK11	15 B1
Holton Cotts.	FK10	19 F2
Holton Cres.	FK10	19 F2
Holton Sq.	FK10	19 F2
Hutton Pk.	FK10	19 F4
Inchna.	FK11	15 B2
INDUSTRIAL ESTATES:		
Alloa Ind Est.	FK10	18 D5
Kelliebank Ind Est.	FK10	18 C5
Inglewood Rd.	FK10	18 C3
Innerdownie Pl.	FK14	21 C1
Izatt Ter.	FK10	20 B5
James Pl.	FK13	Inset 17
James St.	FK12	16 D2
Jamieson Gdns.	FK13	20 B1
Jellyholm Rd.	FK10	19 G3
Johnson Cres.	FK13	20 C1
*Johnstone Ct, West Johnstone St.	FK12	16 C2
Johnstone St, Alva.	FK12	16 D2
Johnstone St, Menstrie.	FK11	15 A1
Katrine Cres.	FK10	19 G5
Keilarsbrae.	FK10	19 F2
Keir Hardie Rd.	FK12	17 E1
Kellie Pl.	FK10	18 D4
Kelliebank.	FK10	18 C5
Kellyburn Pk.	FK14	21 C3
Kent Rd.	FK10	18 C3
Kerse Green Rd.	FK10	20 A5
Keverkae.	FK10	18 D5
Kilncraigs Ct.	FK10	19 F5
Kilncraigs Rd.	FK10	19 F5
King o'Muirs Av.	FK10	16 B4
Kings Ct.	FK10	18 D4
Kingseat Pl.	FK13	20 D1
Kingswell Pk.	FK10	19 F4
Kirk Ct.	FK13	20 C2
Kirk Wynd.	FK10	20 A5
Kirkbrae.	FK10	20 A5
Kirkgate.	FK10	19 E5
Kirkhill Ter.	FK13	20 C2
Kirkstyle Ter.	FK14	21 C2
Kirkstyle.	FK14	21 C2
Kirktoun Gdns.	FK13	20 C2
Lady Ann Gro.	FK13	20 D1
Ladywell Dri.	FK10	15 C4
Ladywell Gro.	FK10	20 A6
Ladywell Pl.	FK10	15 C4
Ladywood.	FK10	20 C6
Lambert Ter.	FK10	19 F4
Langour.	FK13	20 C3
Law Hill Rd.	FK14	21 C2
Lawswell.	FK10	17 G5
Ledi Av.	FK10	15 C6
Lestrange Av.	FK12	16 D1
Leven Ct.	FK10	19 F6
Lewis Ct.	FK10	19 E6
Lilybank Ct.	FK10	19 G2
Lipney.	FK11	15 C2
Lochbrae.	FK10	19 G1
Lochies Rd.	FK10	20 B6
Lomond Ct.	FK10	19 F6
Lomond St.	FK10	18 C2
Long Row.	FK11	15 B1
Lookaboutye Brae.	FK10	20 B6
Lornshill Cres.	FK10	18 C3
Losshill.	FK11	15 C2
Lovers Loan, Alva.	FK12	17 E1
Lovers Loan, Dollar.	FK14	21 C3
Lower Mill St.	FK13	20 A2
Ludgate.	FK10	18 D4
Lychgate Rd.	FK10	15 C6
McKinlay Cres.	FK10	19 F4
Maclean Cres.	FK12	17 E1
McNabb St.	FK14	21 B3
Main St, Tullibody.	FK10	15 D5
Main St, New Sauchie.	FK10	19 F2
Main St, Clackmannan.	FK10	20 B5
Main St, Coalsnaughton.	FK13	Inset 17
Main St East.	FK11	15 B1
Main St West.	FK11	15 A1
Malcolm St.	FK14	21 B3
Mannan Dri.	FK10	20 C6
Manor Cres.	FK10	15 D5
Manor House Rd.	FK14	21 B3
Manse Rd.	FK14	21 C2
Mansfield Av.	FK10	19 G2
Maple Ct.	FK10	19 E5
Mar Pl, Alloa.	FK10	19 E4
Mar Pl, New Sauchie.	FK10	19 F2
Mar St.	FK10	19 E5
Mar Ter.	FK10	20 B5
Marchside Ct.	FK10	19 F2
Maree Ct.	FK10	19 F5
Marquis Dri.	FK10	20 C6
Marshall.	FK10	19 E5
Mary Pl.	FK10	20 A5
Mary Sevenson Dri.	FK10	18 D3
Maxton Cres.	FK12	17 E1
Mayfield Av.	FK13	20 C1
Mayfield Cres.	FK10	20 A5
Meadow Grn.	FK10	19 E2
Meadow Pk.	FK12	16 D2
Medwyn Pl.	FK10	18 C5
Melloch Cres.	FK13	20 C2
Menstrie Pl.	FK11	15 B1
Menstrie. Rd.	FK10	15 D4
Menteith Ct.	FK10	19 F5
Mercat Pl.	FK10	20 C6
Merlin Pk.	FK14	21 C1
Middleton.	FK11	15 C2
Midtown.	FK11	15 B1
Mill Rd, Alloa.	FK10	19 E5
Mill Rd, Clackmannan.	FK10	20 B4
Mill St.	FK10	19 E5
Millars Wynd.	FK10	19 F1
Millbrook Pl.	FK11	15 B1
Minto Ct.	FK12	17 E2
Minto Gdns.	FK12	17 E2
Mitchell Ct.	FK14	21 B3
Mitchell Cres.	FK10	18 C4
Moir St.	FK10	18 D3
Moirs Well.	FK14	21 C1
*Moss Ct, High St.	FK14	21 C2
Moss Rd.	FK13	20 C2
Mount Pleasant.	FK13	Inset 17
Mount William.	FK10	19 H2
Muckhart Rd.	FK14	21 C3
Muircot Pl.	FK13	Inset 17
Muirpark Gdns.	FK10	16 B4
Muirside Rd.	FK10	16 A5
Mull Ct.	FK10	19 E6
Munro Pl.	FK10	18 D5
Murray Pl.	FK14	21 B3
*Murray Sq, Moss Rd.	FK13	20 C2
Mylne Av.	FK14	21 B3
Myreton.	FK11	15 C2
*Myretoungate, Dumyat Rd.	FK12	16 B2
Nevis Cres.	FK10	19 E3
New Brig Rd.	FK10	19 E5
Newbiggin Cres.	FK10	15 D6
Newlands Pl.	FK10	15 D4
Newmills.	FK10	15 C5
Newtonshaw.	FK10	19 F1
North Castle St.	FK10	18 D5
North Hill St.	FK13	20 B1
North St, Alloa.	FK10	18 D4
North St, Clackmannan.	FK10	20 B5
North Wood Rd.	FK10	16 A6
Northfield Gdns.	FK10	20 C6
Norton St.	FK12	16 D2
Norwood Av.	FK10	18 C3
Norwood Cres.	FK10	18 C4
Norwood Gro.	FK10	18 C3
Oberon.	FK10	18 D3
Ochil Ct.	FK10	15 D4
Ochil Rd, Alva.	FK12	16 D1
Ochil Rd, Menstrie.	FK11	15 B1
Ochil St, Alloa.	FK10	18 D4
Ochil St, Tillicoultry.	FK13	20 B1
Ochil St, Tullibody.	FK10	15 D5
Ochil View, Alva.	FK12	16 D1
Ochilview, Tillicoultry.	FK13	20 B3
Ochilview Rd.	FK10	20 B1
Ochivale Ter.	FK10	17 G5
Orkney Ct.	FK10	19 E6
Ormiston Dri.	FK10	18 C1
Park Av.	FK13	20 A2
Park Cres.	FK10	19 F2
*Park La, Park St.	FK13	20 B2
Park Pl, Alloa.	FK10	19 F4
Park Pl, Clackmannan.	FK10	20 B5
Park Pl, Dollar.	FK14	21 C3
Park Rd.	FK11	15 B1
Park St, Alva.	FK12	16 C2
Park St, Coalsnaughton.	FK13	Inset 17
Park St, Tillicoultry.	FK13	20 B2
Park Ter.	FK10	15 C6
Parkgate.	FK12	16 C2
Parkhead Ct.	FK10	19 F3
Parkhead Rd.	FK10	19 F3
Parkway.	FK10	19 E4
Parkway Ct.	FK10	19 E4
Paton St.	FK10	18 D4
Pavillion Vw.	FK10	18 D3
Pennyschool Pl.	FK10	20 B5
Pine Gro.	FK10	19 F5
Pitfairn Rd.	FK10	17 G5
Poachers Grn.	FK10	20 B5
Pompee Rd.	FK10	19 E2
Port St.	FK10	20 A5
Posthill.	FK10	19 G2
Primrose Pl, Alloa.	FK10	19 E4
Primrose Pl, Tillicoultry.	FK13	20 B1
Primrose St.	FK10	19 E4
Princess Cres.	FK14	21 D1
Provost Hunter Av.	FK12	17 E2
Provost Jones Ct.	FK13	20 B1
Quarry Pl.	FK10	19 F3
Queen St, Alloa.	FK10	19 E3
Queen St, Alva.	FK12	16 D1
Ramsay St.	FK13	Inset 17
Ramsay Ter.	FK13	20 C1
Ramsay Tullis Dri.	FK10	15 D6
Rankine Wynd.	FK10	18 A1
Rannoch Ct.	FK10	19 F6
Ravenswood.	FK13	20 C1
Redlands Rd.	FK10	15 C4
Redwell Pl.	FK10	18 C3
Rhodders Gro.	FK12	17 E2
Ring Rd.	FK10	19 E4
Riverside Vw.	FK10	19 E6
Robert Dick Ct.	FK10	15 D6
Robert Kinmond Av.	FK10	15 D6
Robert Knox Av.	FK10	15 D6
Robertson St.	FK12	16 D1
Rose St.	FK10	18 C1
Rosebank.	FK10	19 G2
Rosebank Gdns.	FK10	19 F2
Ross Ct.	FK13	20 C1
Roundelwood, New Sauchie.	FK10	19 E2
Roundelwood, Tillicoultry.	FK13	20 C1
St Leonards.	FK13	20 D1
St Mungos Wynd.	FK10	18 D5
St Serfs Gro.	FK10	20 C6
St Serfs Pl.	FK10	15 C4
St Serfs Rd, Tillicoultry.	FK13	20 C2
St Serfs Rd, Tullibody.	FK10	15 C4
St Serfs Wk.	FK12	16 B2
Sandy Knowe.	FK13	20 D1
Schaw Ct.	FK10	19 G2
Schawpark Av.	FK12	19 G2
School La.	FK11	15 B1
School Rd.	FK10	15 C6
School Ter.	FK13	Inset 17
Scotland Pl.	FK13	20 B1
Scott Cres.	FK10	19 E6
Shaftesbury St.	FK10	18 D4
Sheardale Dri.	FK13	Inset 17
Shetland Ct.	FK10	19 E6
Shillinghill, Alloa.	FK10	19 E5
Shillinghill, Tillicoultry.	FK13	20 B1
Shire Way.	FK10	18 C5
Simpson Av.	FK13	20 D1
Simpson Ct.	FK13	20 D1
Simpson Dri.	FK13	Inset 17
Smiddy Wynd.	FK10	16 D2
Smithfield Loan.	FK10	18 C4
Sorleys Brae.	FK14	21 C2
South Pilmuir Rd.	FK10	20 B6
Southcroft.	FK12	16 C2
Spinners Ct.	FK13	20 C2
Spinners Wynd.	FK13	20 C2
Springfield Rd.	FK10	19 G4
Sprotwell Ter.	FK10	19 G2
Stalker Av.	FK13	20 C1
Stanley Ter.	FK12	16 D2
Stanton Av.	FK10	19 E2
Station Rd, Dollar.	FK14	21 C3
Station Rd, Tullibody.	FK10	15 C6
*Stirling Ct, Stirling St.	FK13	20 B1
Stirling Rd, Alloa.	FK10	18 A2
Stirling Rd, Alva.	FK12	16 D2
Stirling Rd, Stirling St, Alva.	FK10	16 D2
Stirling St, Tullicoultry.	FK13	20 B1
Stoneyacre.	FK13	20 B2
Strachan Cres.	FK14	21 A3
Strathdevon Pl.	FK14	21 C3
Stripehead.	FK10	19 E5
Strude Howe.	FK12	16 D1
Strude Mill.	FK12	16 D1
Strude St.	FK12	17 E1
Sunnyside Ct.	FK10	19 E4
Sunnyside Rd.	FK10	19 E4
Sutherland Av.	FK10	19 F4
Swinburne Dri.	FK10	19 E1
Tarmangie Dri.	FK14	21 C1
Tay Ct.	FK10	19 F5
Ten Acres.	FK10	19 E1
The Baingle.	FK10	15 B5
The Braes.	FK10	16 A5
The Broich.	FK12	16 B1
The Bryony.	FK10	15 C6
The Cairns.	FK11	
The Cedars.	FK10	18 A1
The Cleaves, .	FK10	
The Cloves.	FK11	
The Craigs.	FK13	
The Glebe, Alva.	FK1.	
The Glebe, Clackmannan.	FK10	
The Glebe, Dollar.	FK.	
The Glen, Tillicoultry.	FK13	
The Glen, Coalsnaughton.	FK12	
The Green.	FK12	
The Hennings.	FK10	
The Knowe.	FK10	
The Laurels.	FK10	
The Meadows.	FK13	
The Nebit.	FK12	
The Ness.	FK14	
The Nethergate.	FK10	
The Orchard.	FK10	
The Poplars.	FK10	
The Rowans.	FK10	
The Shore.	FK10	
The Sycamores.	FK10	
The Walk.	FK10	
The Willows.	FK10	
The Wynd.	FK12	
Thistle St.	FK10	
Thompson Pl.	FK13	
Thornbank Rd.	FK14	
Thorne Rd.	FK10	
Titania.	FK10	
Torridon Ct.	FK10	
Torry Dri.	FK12	
Tower Pl.	FK10	
Tower St.	FK10	
Tower Vw.	FK10	
*Tron Ct, Ochil St.	FK10	
Tullibody Rd.	FK10	
Tullich Ter.	FK13	
Tulligarth Pk.	FK10	
Turret Ct.	FK10	
Union St.	FK13	
*Union St, Bank St.	FK10	
Upper Hillfoot Rd.	FK	
Upper Mill St.	FK13	
Victoria St.	FK10	
Victoria Ter.	FK11	
Viewfield Dri.	FK12	
Walker Ter.	FK13	
Wallace St.	FK10	
Wallace Vw.	FK10	
Walnut Pk.	FK13	
Walton Cres.	FK14	
Ward St.	FK10	
Wardlaw St.	FK13	
Weavers Way.	FK13	
Wellmyre.	FK10	
West Burnside.	FK14	
West End Gdns.	FK10	
West James St.	FK12	
West Johnstone St.	FK	
West Lodge Gdns.	FK1	
West Stirling St.	FK12	
West Vennel.	FK10	
Westbourne Av.	FK10	
Westview Cres.	FK10	
Wharry Rd.	FK12	
Whins Rd.	FK10	
White Wisp Gdns.	FK	
Windsor Gdns.	FK10	
Windsor St.	FK11	
Wood Avens.	FK10	
Woodburn Dri.	FK10	
Woodburn Way.	FK12	
Woodhead Pl.	FK13	
Woodlands.	FK10	
Woodlea Gdns.	FK10	
Woodlea Pk.	FK10	
Woodside Rd, Alloa.	FK10	
Woodside Rd, Tullibody.	FK10	
Woodside Ter.	FK10	
Zetland St.	FK10	